W9-AYU-938

How Do You Live There?

LIVING IN THE ARCTIC

Alicia Z. Klepeis

PowerKiDS
press™

NEW YORK

Published in 2021 by The Rosen Publishing Group, Inc.
29 East 21st Street, New York, NY 10010

Copyright © 2021 by The Rosen Publishing Group, Inc.

Editor: Kristen Susienka
Designer: Rachel Rising

Photo Credits: Cover, Denis Belitsky/Shutterstock.com; Back Cover, pp. 3,5,6,8,10,12,13,14,16,18,19, 20,21,22,23,24,26,27,28,30,31,32 (background) Yevhenii Borshosh/Shutterstock.com; p. 5 https://commons. wikimedia.org/wiki/File:Arctic_circle.svg; p, 7 Jan Miko/Shutterstock.com; p.9 Peter Hermes Furian/Shutterstock. com; p. 11 longtaildog/Shutterstock.com; p. 13 gor_C/Shutterstock.com; p. 15 https://en.wikipedia.org/wiki/ Snow_goggles#/media/File:Inuit_snow_goggles.jpg; p. 17 Vova Shevchuk/Shutterstock.com; p. 18 Olga Gavrilova/ Shutterstock.com; p, 19 Chris Christophersen/Shutterstock.com; p. 20 Ondrej Prosicky/Shutterstock.com; p. 21 ginger_ polina_bublik/Shutterstock.com; p. 23 Delpixel/Shutterstock.com; p. 25 Yongyut Kumsri/Shutterstock.com; p. 27 Jan Martin Will/Shutterstock.com; p.29 GABRIEL BOUYS/AFP/Getty Images; p. 30 Stefan Auth/Getty Images.

Library of Congress Cataloging-in-Publication Data

Names: Klepeis, Alicia, 1971- author. | PowerKids Press.
Title: Living in the Arctic / Alicia Z. Klepeis.
Description: New York : PowerKids Press, 2020. | Series: How do you live
    there?! | Includes index.
Identifiers: LCCN 2019045498 | ISBN 9781725316447 (Paperback) | ISBN
    9781725316461 (Library Binding) | ISBN 9781725316454 (6 pack)
Subjects: LCSH: Arctic regions--Juvenile literature.
Classification: LCC G614 .K54 2020 | DDC 909/.0913--dc23
LC record available at https://lccn.loc.gov/2019045498

Manufactured in the United States of America

Some of the images in this book illustrate individuals who are models. The depictions do not imply actual situations or events.

CPSIA Compliance Information: Batch #CSPK20. For further information contact Rosen Publishing, New York, New York at 1-800-237-9932.

Find us on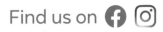

The Arctic is located at the top of the planet. Some think of the Arctic as everything north of the Arctic Circle. Others think it also includes the land just south of the Arctic Circle. The Arctic Circle is an imaginary line that circles Earth about 66.5 degrees north of the **equator**. Eight countries have land in the Arctic: Norway, Sweden, Finland, Russia, Canada, the United States, Iceland, and Greenland. Polar bears, the North Pole, snow, and ice are in the Arctic.

Water covers most of the Arctic. Much of it is frozen in ice sheets. Large areas of the sea in the Arctic are frozen as sea ice. Smaller blocks of ice called icebergs also float in the water. Some areas of land are covered by masses of ice called glaciers. Glaciers form mountains and valleys over time.

North Pacific
Ocean

ALEUTIAN ISLANDS

Bering Sea

Petropavlovsk-
Kamchatskiy

occupied by the Soviet Union in 1945,
administered by Russia, claimed by Japan.

KURIL ISL.

JA

Sakhalin

Sea of
Okhotsk

Khabarov

Amur

Kodiak

Bethel

Gulf of
Alaska

Anchorage
Valdez

UNITED STATES
Nome

Bering
Strait

Providentya Anadyr'

Magadan

Okhotsk

Juneau

Whitehorse

Fairbanks

Arctic Circle

Chukchi
Sea

Pevek

Cherskiy

Oymyakon

Yakutsk

Amur

Dawson

Wrangel
Island

East
Siberian
Sea

Verkhoyansk

Watson
Lake

Prudhoe
Bay

Barrow

average minimum
extent of sea ice

Tiksi

Hay
River

Inuvik

Mackenzie River

Great Bear
Lake

Beaufort
Sea

NEW
SIBERIAN
ISLANDS

Laptev
Sea

Echo Bay
Yellowknife

Great Slave
Lake

Banks
Island

80

SEVERNAYA
ZEMLYA

10°C (50°F) isothe
July

Victoria
Island

Arctic
Ocean

Noril'sk

Cambridge
Bay

CANADA

QUEEN
ELIZABETH
ISLANDS

North
Pole

RUSSIA

Kångiqcliniq
(Rankin Inlet)

Kaujuitoq
(Resolute)

Dikson

FRANZ
JOSEF
LAND

Kara
Sea

Repulse Bay

Ellesmere
Island

Alert

Baffin
Island

Qaanaaq
(Thule)

80

NOVAYA
ZEMLYA

Iqaluit
(Frobisher Bay)

Baffin
Bay

Nord

Longyearbyen

Svalbard
(NORWAY)

Barents Sea

Davis Strait

Greenland
(DENMARK)

Kangerlussuaq
(Søndre Strømfjord)

Bjørnøya
(NORWAY)

Murmansk

Nuuk
(Godthåb)

Itseqqortoormiit
(Scoresbysund)

Greenland
Sea

Arkhangel'sk

Paamiut
(Frederikshåb)

Tasiilaq
(Ammassalik)

Narsarsuaq

Jan Mayen
(NORWAY)

Tromsø

Perm

Kazan'

Lake
Onega

Severnaya Dvina

Labrador
Sea

Denmark Strait

Norwegian
Sea

Arctic Circle

ICELAND

Reykjavík

Faroe
Islands
(DENMARK)

North Atlantic Ocean

Torshavn

SHETLAND
ISLANDS

NORWAY

SWEDEN

Oslo

FINLAND

Helsinki

Stockholm

Tallinn

EST.

Lake
Ladoga

St. Petersburg

Nizhniy
Novgorod

Moscow

Saratov

Sa

Vo

Scale 1:39,000,000
Azimuthal Equal-Area Projection

0   500 Kilometers

500 Miles

LATVIA

Riga

Baltic
Sea

RUS.

Vilnius
LITH.

Minsk

BELARUS

Copenhagen

North

Kharkiv

Ros

5

The Arctic has different landscapes. Islands and **fjords** dot the region. There are mountains, like the Brooks Range in Alaska. Siberia, a part of Russia, has river valleys and grassy **plateaus**. Most of Greenland is covered in a giant sheet of ice, even though its name makes you think it's not!

The Arctic has different seasons, but it is usually chilly. In summer, the average temperature is around 50°Fahrenheit (10°Celsius). In winter, though, temperatures can drop below −50°F (−46°C).

Northernmost areas in the Arctic may have permanent ice and snow. Some areas have **permafrost**. This is where the ground is always frozen. In summer, the top layer may thaw, but the soil underneath stays frozen.

Wildlife in the Arctic

Despite the cold, plants and animals live in the Arctic. Grasses and small bushes grow near the southern edges of the Arctic. Flowers, lichens, and mosses also grow on rocks and in fields in parts of the Arctic. Seals, walruses, and whales swim in the water. Reindeer, musk oxen, and Arctic foxes live on land. Polar bears live and hunt on the Arctic sea ice. They all have **adapted** to life in a tough place.

Icebergs dot the surface of Jökulsárlón glacial lagoon in southeastern Iceland.

Earth spins on an invisible **axis**. This axis is tilted. As a result, the sun's rays hit different places on Earth more strongly at certain times of the year. When it's winter north of the equator, the Arctic is very cold and dark. During summer, the Arctic receives lots of sunlight.

The longest and shortest days of the year are called **solstices**. On the summer solstice in the nothern hemisphere, everywhere above the Arctic Circle has one full day of sunshine. On the winter solstice, the sun never rises, and there is one full day of darkness. However, the northern parts of the Arctic are dark for *months* during the winter. This is called a polar night. It usually lasts from November to January.

The Arctic Explored

Native peoples have lived in the Arctic for thousands of years. However, this region was unknown to the rest of the world for a long time. In the 1500s, Europeans began trying to explore the Arctic. Between 1908 and 1909, American explorer Robert E. Peary led a trip to the North Pole. He had learned many helpful tips from the native people living in Greenland. Today, people aren't sure if Peary and his team actually reached the North Pole. They definitely got very close.

During the Northern Hemisphere's winter solstice, the North Pole is tilted away from the sun. It is dark all day above the Arctic Circle, and light all day below the Antarctic Circle.

WINTER SOLSTICE

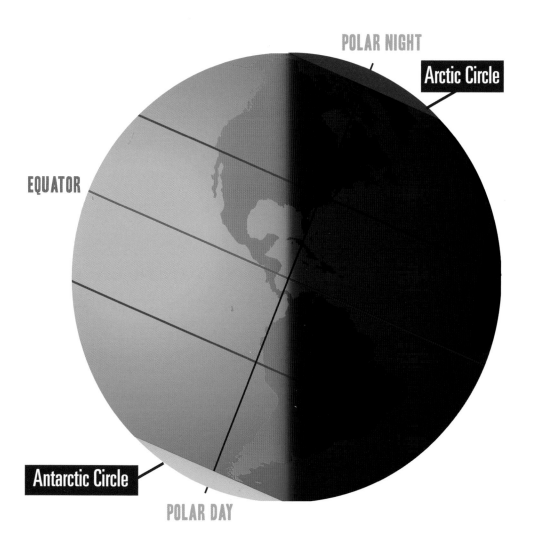

POLAR NIGHT

Arctic Circle

EQUATOR

Antarctic Circle

POLAR DAY

NATIVE GROUPS OF THE ARCTIC

During winter, Arctic temperatures and winds are dangerously cold. In order to go outside, people who live there must wear the right clothes. Strong winds and heavy snowfall during storms can also make travel tough. Heating buildings is challenging. Many times, groceries have to be flown in and delivered in cold temperatures. Yet people have adapted to life here.

Today, more than 40 native groups live in the Arctic. For example, the Sami people live in Norway, Sweden, Finland, and Russia. The Inuit live in Canada, Greenland, and Alaska. The Nenets are from Siberia. Most of the Evenk people also come from Siberia. These native peoples learned to survive in the Arctic's harsh environment.

This winter camp includes the housing, sleds, and other belongings of an Arctic tribe. Tents like this are easy to put up and take down, allowing the tribe to move from place to place. ▶

FINDING FOOD

Native Arctic peoples traditionally fished, hunted, and herded. To catch their food, they used tools they made from rocks, whale bone, or other animal parts. They also gathered wild plants. Meat and fish were the most important food sources. Whales were very prized, and Arctic natives who hunted them used almost every part.

The Sami ate mostly reindeer meat and fish. Both animals have lots of **protein**. The Sami people grilled, boiled, dried, salted, or smoked their fish. Wild berries like cloudberries gave them energy and important vitamins.

The Inuit mostly ate meat they hunted. This included seals, walruses, arctic hares, and more. The Inuit also ate fish. Whitefish, salmon, and arctic char were common. During summer, they collected berries and other plants.

Today, Arctic fishermen sail the waters in boats like this one. ➡

Use What You've Got!

Arctic fishermen and hunters made their hunting tools from the environment in which they lived. The Inuit people made fishing nets from animal sinew. This is tough tissue that connects muscle to bone. They did not waste any parts of the animals they hunted. Arctic people made fishing hooks from wood, bone, antlers, and animal claws. Sometimes they also carved artworks from these different animal parts.

ARCTIC CLOTHING

Arctic peoples wore many layers to keep them safe from the cold. The more layers a person wore, the warmer they would be. Most Arctic clothing was made from animal skins and furs. The Inuit used caribou skin to make clothes. Why? It was lightweight, but it kept people warm! Clothing was also made from sealskin and polar bear skin.

Arctic women and men wore similar clothing: pants, parkas, mittens, and boots. A woman's parka was a big, furry coat. They called it an *amauti*. It had a special hood that was large enough to carry a baby or a small child. Some native groups made snow goggles from caribou antlers, animal bones, or walrus tusks to protect their eyes from wintry weather. Some of these clothing traditions continue today.

An Inuit man wears snow goggles to protect his eyes against snow blindness in the Arctic. ➡

AT HOME IN THE ARCTIC

Thick layers of snow cover the Arctic for most of the year. Many areas don't have trees available to cut down. Arctic native peoples had to come up with ways to build shelters out of whatever they could find.

One kind of Inuit house was the igloo, or snow house. People built these dome-shaped homes from stacked, rectangular blocks of snow. The blocks kept out the wind and cold. The walls trapped warm air inside. People used animal furs as beds. Up to 20 people could live in one igloo.

Some Arctic peoples lived in tents. The Sami used wood poles from the **taiga** to hold up their tents. People covered the tents with animal skins. The skins kept out the cold weather and strong winds.

The Inuit often build igloos as brief winter homes or to give shelter during hunting trips. ⟶

MODERN LIFE

Millions of people live in the Arctic today. Many live in modern cities and towns. Others live in small villages, and some even live just as their ancestors did hundreds of years ago.

The most populous city north of the Arctic Circle is Murmansk, Russia. Close to 300,000 people live there. This city was originally a military supply port during World War I. Today, it is an important economic port in Russia. Industries in Murmansk include fishing, fish processing, and shipbuilding.

These colorful homes are located in the village of Saqqaq in western Greenland.

On the other hand, less than 3,000 people live in Jokkmokk. It is a small community in Sweden. Herders here watch over hundreds of reindeer. The winter market in Jokkmokk has been going on for over 400 years!

There are many jobs in the Arctic. Mining is an important one. The Arctic has lots of natural gas and oil. There are also minerals and metals like copper and nickel. Mining is challenging in the Arctic. Some minerals lie beneath the Arctic Ocean or in the frozen ground. Mining machines sometimes freeze. The frozen ground can make it impossible to drill.

Fishing and hunting are common jobs. Sometimes people fish for their families. Larger companies also fish here. Salmon, cod, and crab are caught in the Arctic.

Snow-covered mountains and blue ice are part of the amazing scenery of Norway's Svalbard Islands

These trucks are helping to load coal at a mine in Longyearbyen, Norway.

Arctic tourism is growing. Visitors from around the world come to see Iceland's volcanoes and waterfalls. Local people in Greenland can take the country's Adventure Guides course. This training helps them share their homeland with tourists.

GETTING AROUND

Transportation in the Arctic has changed from what it once was. In the past, groups traveled by sleds pulled by dogs or reindeer. Some people even traveled many miles using snowshoes.

Today, a traditional dog sled race called the Iditarod takes teams on a route over the snow and ice of Alaska. However, many newer transportation technologies now help people living in cold parts of the world get from place to place. Snowmobiles and airplanes are popular ways to travel. Trains also take tourists to the Arctic.

Icebreakers are important to Arctic travel. These super-powerful ships can break up thick sea ice. This means people and goods can get to hard-to-reach places. Airplanes also deliver food and other supplies to the Arctic.

Tourists go snowmobiling in Saariselkä, a town located 155 miles (250 km) north of the Arctic Circle in Finland. ⊢━━━➤

Pond Inlet's Hockey Team

Hockey is a popular Arctic activity. The Pond Inlet hockey team in Nunavut, Canada, is famous because it has to travel by snowmobile for at least 24 hours to play against other teams! They fill sleds attached to the snowmobiles with their sticks, jerseys, and skates. They also bring tents and extra gasoline. They can't set an exact time for a hockey game. Why? They are never quite sure how long it will take to reach the other team!

BUILDING TECHNOLOGY

Just as ancient peoples adapted to their surroundings, people today are developing new technologies to deal with the Arctic weather. Buildings have improved over time by getting better insulation. Some have heated floors. People can even get an Arctic construction degree!

Permafrost continues to be a challenge. The ground can soften in the spring when the permafrost thaws. This can cause buildings to shift. Some homes have metal posts called pilings that hold them up. These pilings have special screws. They help adjust a building's **foundation** until it's level with the ground.

The Inuit community of Iqaluit, Canada, has installed special pumps into the foundations of bigger buildings. The pumps draw heat from the land. This helps keep permafrost cold. As a result, buildings are less likely to sink or move.

These homes are in Qeqertarsuaq, a port town of about 860 people on Greenland's Disko Island. ⊢———⟶

THE THREAT OF A MELTING ARCTIC

Think of the Arctic as Earth's refrigerator. The ice and snow in the Arctic region reflect sunlight back into space. This means the Arctic absorbs less heat from the sun. This helps keep Earth cool. Unfortunately, **climate change** is having a big impact on the Arctic.

Warmer temperatures are causing Arctic ice to melt. The sea ice is shrinking. This can hurt many Arctic animals. For example, polar bears need sea ice to rest, hunt, eat their meals, and find mates. Without it, they might not survive.

If the ice melts, it would be easier for big ships to travel around the Arctic. This might seem like a good thing. However, big ships could make it more difficult for fishermen and hunters with small boats to work and get around.

A polar bear searches for food while drifting on a piece of ice in the Arctic. ⊢⟶

Polar Bear Problems

Thanks to climate change, sea ice is melting. This means polar bears and walruses are struggling to find food. In February 2019, a village in the Russian Arctic was taken over by more than 50 polar bears looking for food. Some even entered buildings. This is dangerous for both the bears and people. Some Arctic communities have started polar bear patrols. They warn people if bears are close.

EROSION TECH AND LOOKING TO THE FUTURE

Climate change causes many problems. One is the thawing of permafrost. Another is the melting of sea ice. This makes the ocean water rough and causes **erosion**. Climate change can also lead to strong winds, storms, and flooding.

One way to deal with erosion and storms is to design movable homes. One idea is to have a house built on skis. That would allow people to move the house if the ocean water gets too close.

People are smart. Long ago, native peoples learned how to live in the Arctic. Today, technology is always improving. It is getting easier for more people to live in harsh environments like the Arctic. It's likely that people will call the Arctic home for a very long time.

In 2006, beach erosion destroyed this home in the Alaskan coastal village of Shishmaref.

EARTH'S MOST NORTHERLY COMMUNITIES

CITY	LATITUDE/LONGITUDE	POPULATION
Pyramiden, Norway	78°39'22"N / 16°19'30"E	4 to 15
Longyearbyen, Norway	78°13'00"N / 15°33'00"E	about 2,000
Barentsburg, Norway	78°04'00"N / 14°13'00"E	470
Qaanaaq, Greenland	77°29'N / 69°20'W	656
Grise Fiord, Canada	76°25'N / 82°53'W	130
Resolute, Canada	74°41'N / 94°49'W	about 230

Pyramiden, Norway

GLOSSARY

adapt: To change in order to live better in a certain environment.

axis: An imaginary straight line around which a body in space turns.

climate change: Changes in Earth's weather patterns caused by human activity.

equator: An imaginary line that circles Earth and divides it into two equal areas—the northern and southern hemispheres.

erosion: The wearing away of Earth's surface by wind or water.

fjord: A narrow inlet of the sea between cliffs or steep slopes.

foundation: A base, usually made of stone or concrete, that supports a building.

permafrost: A layer of soil that is always frozen in very cold areas of the world.

plateau: A large, flat area of land that is higher than other areas of land that surround it.

protein: A substance found in some foods (such as meat, milk, eggs, and beans) that is important for growth and health.

solstice: The day of the year when the sun passes overhead the farthest north (summer solstice, about June 22) or south (winter solstice, about December 22) of the equator.

taiga: An environmental region located just south of the tundra and covered largely with coniferous trees such as firs and spruces.

INDEX

A
adaptation, 6, 10, 16, 24, 28
Alaska, 6, 10, 22, 29
Arctic Circle, 4, 8, 9, 18, 22

B
buildings, 10, 16, 24, 28

C
Canada, 4, 10, 23, 24, 30
climate change, 26, 27, 28
clothing, 10, 14

E
erosion, 28, 29
explorers, 8

F
Finland, 4, 10, 22
fishing, 12, 13, 18, 20, 26
fjords, 6
food, 12, 22

G
glaciers, 4
Greenland, 4, 6, 8, 10, 18,
    19, 21, 24, 30

H
hockey, 23
hunting, 6, 12, 13, 16,
    20, 26

I
icebergs, 4, 7
icebreakers, 22
Iceland, 4, 7, 21
Iditarod, 22
igloo, 16
Inuit, 10, 12, 13, 14,
    16, 24

M
mining, 20, 21
mountains, 4, 6, 20
Murmansk, 18

N
North Pole, 4, 8, 9
Norway, 4, 10, 20, 21, 30

P
permafrost, 6, 24, 28
plants, 6, 12, 16
plateaus, 6
polar bears, 4, 6, 14, 26, 27
polar night, 8, 9

R
reindeer, 6, 12, 19, 22
Russia, 4, 6, 10, 18, 27

S
Sami, 10, 12, 16
sea ice, 4, 6, 22, 26, 27, 28
sleds, 10, 22, 23
snowmobiles, 22, 23
solstice, 8, 9
Sweden, 4, 10, 19

T
tents, 10, 16, 23
transportation, 12, 22,
    23, 26

W
walruses, 6, 12, 14, 27
whales, 6, 12
wind, 10, 16, 28

WEBSITES

Due to the changing nature of Internet links, PowerKids Press has developed an online list of websites related to the subject of this book. This site is updated regularly. Please use this link to access the list:
www.powerkidslinks.com/hdylt/arctic